D0560036

LIFE'S LITTLE TREASURE BOOK

On Success

H. JACKSON BROWN, JR.

RUTLEDGE HILL PRESS

NASHVILLE, TENNESSEE

Published in Nashville, Tennessee, by
Rutledge Hill Press, Inc., 211 Seventh Avenue
North, Nashville, Tennessee 37219.
Distributed in Canada by H. B. Fenn and
Company, Ltd., Mississauga, Ontario.

Typography by D&T/Bailey Typesetting, Inc.,
Nashville, Tennessee
Illustrations by Cristine Mortensen
Book design by Harriette Bateman

ISBN: 1-55853-280-3

Printed in Hong Kong through Palace Press
2 3 4 5 6 7 8 9 — 97 96 95 94

INTRODUCTION

$\mathcal{T}$here are two ways to judge success: from our own measure and from the evaluation of others.

Concerning the first view, I've always been inspired by Bessie Anderson Stanley's observation that "He has achieved success who has lived well, laughed often, and loved much." My father had his own idea. "Judge your success," he advised, "by measuring how far you've come with the talents you've been given." His words were a reminder that a successful life doesn't require that we've done *the* best, but that we've done *our* best.

We often lose sight of this and begin to compare our lives with others. Unfortunately, this often ends in envy, frustration, and disappointment.

This little book is a collection of my observations about success that I shared with my son, Adam, in both volumes of *Life's Little Instruction Book*. Thought-provoking and inspiring

quotes from other sources are also
included.

You will find no new revelations
here. Self-discipline, integrity,
kindness, and courage are still the
secrets to successful living.

Once again, mom was right.

Commit yourself to quality.

∽

There are people who will
always come up with reasons
why you can't do what
you want to do. Ignore them.

$\mathcal{W}$atch your attitude.
It's the first thing people
notice about you.

❧

$\mathcal{W}$hen you find someone
doing small things well,
put him or her in charge of
bigger things.

A racehorse that consistently runs just a second faster than another horse is worth millions of dollars more. Be willing to give that extra effort that separates the winner from the one in second place.

Don't be called out on strikes.
Go down swinging.

❧

Thunder is good,
thunder is impressive;
but it is the lightning
that does the work.

—Mark Twain

$\mathcal{B}$e punctual and insist
on it in others.

∾

$\mathcal{S}$hare the credit.

∾

$\mathcal{G}$et acquainted with a good
lawyer, accountant,
and plumber.

It's no use saying,
"We are doing our best."
You have got to succeed
in doing what
is necessary.

— Winston Churchill

Set high goals for
your employees and
help them attain them.

❧

Choose a business partner
the way you choose a
tennis partner.
Select someone who's strong
where you are weak.

When you arrive at your job
in the morning,
let the first thing you say
brighten everyone's day.

❧

Do your homework
and know your facts,
but remember it's passion
that persuades.

$\mathcal{L}$ook for ways to make
your boss look good.

❧

$\mathcal{B}$uy and use your
customers' products.

❧

$\mathcal{K}$eep your watch
five minutes fast.

I'm opposed to
millionaires, but
it would be dangerous to
offer me the position.

— Mark Twain

❧

When opportunity knocks,
invite it to stay for dinner.

Never ask a lawyer
or accountant for
business advice.
They are trained to
find problems,
not solutions.

❧

Never be photographed with
a cocktail glass in your hand.

*L*earn how to read
a financial report.

❧

*P*ay your bills on time.

❧

*I*n business or in life,
don't follow the
wagon tracks too closely.

Conduct yourself in
such a way that your
high school would want
you to address the
graduating seniors.

∾

Never hire someone
you wouldn't invite
home to dinner.

Judge your success
by the degree that
you're enjoying
peace, health, and love.

∽

Never waste an opportunity
to tell good employees
how much they mean
to the company.

The man who wakes up and finds himself a success hasn't been asleep.

—Anonymous

$\mathcal{D}$on't be surprised to
discover that luck favors
those who are prepared.

∾

$\mathcal{U}$se credit cards
only for convenience,
never for credit.

*C*hoose work that is
in harmony with your values.

❧

*B*e enthusiastic about
the success of others.

❧

*D*on't discuss
personal matters with
business associates.

*W*hen paying cash,
ask for a discount.

❧

*T*alk slow but
think quick.

❧

*P*ay attention to
the details.

Get a haircut a week before
the big interview.

❧

Never forget that
only dead fish swim
with the stream.

— Malcolm Muggeridge

When you go to borrow money, dress as if you have plenty of it.

❧

Think twice before deciding not to charge for your work. People often don't value what they don't pay for.

*D*on't discuss business
in elevators.
You never know who
may overhear you.

❧

*I*nstead of using
the word *problem*,
try substituting
the word *opportunity*.

Answer the phone with
enthusiasm and energy
in your voice.

❧

Be original.

*W*hen facing a difficult task,
act as though it is
impossible to fail.
If you're going after
Moby Dick, take along
the tartar sauce.

❧

*D*on't mistake motion
for efficiency.

Commit yourself
to constant
self-improvement.

$\mathcal{D}$on't waste time grieving
over past mistakes.
Learn from them
and move on.

❧

$\mathcal{R}$emember that a person
who is foolish with money is
foolish in other ways too.

*B*e a leader.
Remember the lead sled dog is
the only one with
a decent view.

∾

*K*eep expectations high.

∾

*K*eep overhead low.

$\mathcal{D}$on't be a person who says,
"Ready, fire, aim."

∾

$\mathcal{D}$on't be a person who says,
"Ready, aim, aim, aim."

∾

$\mathcal{F}$ollow your own star.

*W*hen concluding a
business deal and the
other person suggests working
out the details later, say,
"I understand, but
I would like to settle the
entire matter right now."
Don't move from the table
until you do.

$\mathcal{E}$nter a room like you
own the place.

❧

$\mathcal{S}$eek opportunity,
not security.
A boat in a harbor is safe,
but in time its bottom
will rot out.

$\mathcal{R}$ead between the lines.

❧

$\mathcal{L}$earn the rules.
Then break some.

❧

$\mathcal{D}$on't be thin-skinned.
Take criticism as well as
praise with equal grace.

Read carefully anything
that requires your signature.
Remember the big print
giveth and the small print
taketh away.

*W*ear out,
don't rust out.

❧

*Y*ou may be fortunate and
make a lot of money.
But be sure your work
involves something that
enriches your spirit as well as
your bank account.

$\mathcal{M}$ind the store.
No one cares about
your business
the way you do.

❧

$\mathcal{E}$very now and then,
bite off more than
you can chew.

*W*hether it's life or
a horse that throws you,
get right back on.

❧

*Y*our mind can hold only
one thought at a time.
Make it a positive and
constructive one.

*T*hink twice before
accepting a job that
requires you to work in an
office with no windows.

❧

*T*ake charge of your attitude.
Don't let someone else
choose it for you.

When there's a piano
to be moved,
don't reach for the stool.

✌

Focus on making things
better, not bigger.

$\mathcal{D}$on't accept
"good enough"
as good enough.

❧

$\mathcal{A}$cquire things the
old-fashioned way:
Save for them and pay cash.

When talking to the press,
remember they always have
the last word.

❧

Decide to get up
thirty minutes earlier.
Do this for a year, and you will
add seven and one-half days to
your waking world.

$\mathcal{N}$ever resist a temporary inconvenience if it results in a permanent improvement.

$\mathcal{N}$ever apologize for
being early for
an appointment.

∾

$\mathcal{G}$et your priorities straight.
No one ever said
on his deathbed,
"Gee, if I'd only spent
more time at the office."

$\mathcal{L}$ook for opportunities to
make people feel important.

∾

$\mathcal{D}$on't confuse wealth
with success.

∾

$\mathcal{D}$on't quit a job until
you've lined up another.

If you want to do something
and you feel in your bones that
it's the right thing to do,
do it. Intuition is often as
important as the facts.

∾

*G*ive your clients your
enthusiastic best.

Stop blaming others.
Take responsibility
for every area of
your life.

∾

Go the distance.
When you accept a task,
finish it.

When starting out,
don't worry about not
having enough money.
Limited funds are
a blessing, not a curse.
Nothing encourages
creative thinking in
quite the same way.

$\mathcal{D}$iscipline yourself
to save money.
It's essential to success.

∾

$\mathcal{N}$ever give up on what
you really want to do.
The person with big dreams
is more powerful than
one with all the facts.

$\mathcal{V}$olunteer.
Sometimes the jobs
no one wants conceal
big opportunities.

❧

$\mathcal{G}$rind it out.
Hanging on just one second
longer than your competition
makes you the winner.

*P*erform your job
better than anyone else can.
That's the best job security
I know.

❧

*R*emember
the deal's not done
until the check has
cleared the bank.

*I*nstead of using the words,
if only, try substituting
the words, *next time.*

∾

*B*e a self-starter.

∾

*S*et short-term and
long-term goals.

*P*romise big.
Deliver big.

❧

*D*on't delay acting on
a good idea. Chances are
someone else has just thought
of it too. Success comes to
the one who acts first.

*G*et organized.
If you don't know
where to start, read
Stephanie Winston's
Getting Organized
(Warner Books, 1978).

❧

*B*e willing to lose a battle
in order to win the war.

*J*udge your success
by what you had
to give up
in order to
get it.

*F*orget committees.
New, noble,
world-changing ideas
always come from
one person
working alone.

∾

*A*sk for a raise when
you feel you've earned it.

When you find a job
that's ideal, take it
regardless of the pay.
If you've got what it takes,
your salary will soon
reflect your value to
the company.

∾

Deadlines are important.
Meet them.

*K*eep a diary of
your accomplishments at work.
Then when you ask for a raise,
you'll have the information
you need to back it up.

ॐ

*D*on't flaunt your success,
but don't apologize
for it either.

$\mathcal{D}$emand excellence and
be willing to pay for it.

❧

$\mathcal{D}$o it right the first time.

Some things need doing
better than they've ever
been done before.
Some just need doing.
Others don't need doing at all.
Know which is which.

Spend your time and energy
creating, not criticizing.

$\mathscr{B}$e decisive
even if it means
you'll sometimes
be wrong.

∞

$\mathscr{N}$o matter what
accomplishments you make,
somebody helps you.

— Althea Gibson

*R*emember that
just the moment you say,
"I give up,"
someone else seeing the
same situation is saying,
"My, what a great
opportunity."

∾

*B*e quick to take advantage
of an advantage.

*M*ake a habit of
reading something
inspiring and cheerful
just before
going to sleep.

Try not to become a man of success but rather try to become a man of values.

— Albert Einstein

$\mathcal{L}$earn to save on
even the most modest salary.
If you do, you're almost
assured of financial success.

❧

$\mathcal{E}$very day look for
some small way to
improve the way
you do your job.

$\mathcal{D}$on't say you
don't have enough time.
You have exactly the same
number of hours per day
that were given to
Helen Keller, Louis Pasteur,
Michelangelo, Mother Teresa,
Leonardo da Vinci,
Thomas Jefferson, and
Albert Einstein.

*A*rrive at work early and
stay beyond quitting time.

❧

*H*ire people
smarter than you.

$\mathcal{R}$emember the
old proverb,
"Out of debt,
out of danger."

❧

$\mathcal{D}$on't do business with
anyone who has a
history of
suing people.

*W*ork hard to create in
your children a
good self-image.
It's the most important thing
you can do to
ensure their success.

❧

*R*ead *Leadership Is an Art*
by Max De Pree (Dell, 1989).

$\mathcal{W}$atch for
big problems.
They disguise
big opportunities.

$\mathcal{D}$on't think people at the
top of their professions have
all the answers.
They don't.

∾

$\mathcal{S}$eize every
opportunity for
additional training in
your job.

$\mathcal{B}$e prepared to lose
once in a while.

❧

$\mathcal{N}$ever risk what you
can't afford to lose.

❧

$\mathcal{D}$on't waste time learning the
"tricks of the trade."
Instead, learn the trade.

*I want to be thoroughly
used up when I die.
Life is no brief candle to me;
it is a sort of splendid torch
which I get ahold of for the
moment and I want to make it
burn as brightly as possible
before handing it on to
future generations.*

— George Bernard Shaw

$\mathcal{D}$on't work for a
company led by someone
of questionable character.

❧

*Take calculated risks.
This is quite different
from being rash.*

— George S. Patton

If you work for
an organization that
makes its decisions
by committee,
make darn sure you're
on the committee.

❧

Learn to listen.
Opportunity sometimes
knocks very softly.

$\mathcal{B}$ecome an expert in
time management.

❧

$\mathcal{B}$e open to new ideas.

❧

$\mathcal{Q}$uestion your goals by asking,
"Will this help me
become my very best?"

When negotiating your salary,
think of what you want;
then ask for 10 percent more.

∾

Start every day with
the most important thing
you have to do.
Save the less important
tasks for later.

*Knowing is not enough,
we must apply.
Willing is not enough,
we must do.*

— Goethe

$\mathcal{B}$e better prepared than
you think you will
need to be.

～

$\mathcal{K}$eep several irons in the fire.

～

$\mathcal{S}$trive for excellence,
not perfection.

$\mathscr{R}$emember that
overnight success
usually takes
about fifteen years.

❧

$\mathscr{K}$eep a note pad and pencil
on your bedside table.
Million-dollar ideas
sometimes strike at 3:00 A.M.

$\mathcal{L}$et your handshake
be as binding as a
signed contract.

$\mathcal{B}$e advised that
when negotiating,
if you don't get it in writing,
you probably won't get it.

∾

$\mathcal{S}$ee problems as
opportunities for
growth and self-mastery.

$\mathcal{R}$emember that
winners do what
losers don't want to do.

∾

$\mathcal{D}$o a good job
because you want to,
not because you have to.
This puts you in charge
instead of your boss.

Take care of your reputation. It's your most valuable asset.

$\mathcal{B}$ecome famous for
finishing important,
difficult tasks.

∾

$\mathcal{K}$now how to type.

∾

$\mathcal{R}$emain open,
flexible, curious.

*I*mprove your performance
by improving your attitude.

❧

*D*on't make the same
mistake twice.

❧

*S*ave 10 percent of
what you earn.

$\mathcal{B}$ecome the kind of person who brightens a room just by entering it.

❧

$\mathcal{D}$on't think expensive equipment will make up for lack of talent or practice.

*H*ave a will and
tell your next-of-kin
where it is.

∿

*N*ever sign contracts with
blank spaces.

Live your life so that
your epitaph could read,
"No regrets."

❧

If you need to bring in
a business partner,
make sure he or she
brings along
some money.

$\mathcal{D}$on't procrastinate.
Do what needs doing
when it needs to be done.

❦

$\mathcal{G}$ive your best to
your employer.
It's one of the
best investments
you can make.

*D*on't let anyone talk you
out of pursuing what
you know to be
a great idea.

∾

*B*e prepared.
You never get a
second chance to make a
good first impression.

$\mathcal{G}$ive people
more than they expect
and do it cheerfully.

∾

$\mathcal{A}$fter you've worked hard
to get what you want,
take the time to
enjoy it.